Louise
Park

Sudanthi

craft
attack

Programmed
craft for the
frenzied teacher

ASHTON SCHOLASTIC
SYDNEY AUCKLAND NEW YORK TORONTO LONDON

Quilled paper designs

What you need

coloured paper strips
bobby pins
PVA glue

What to do

1 Cut the tips off the ends of the pins.
2 Slide the end of the paper strip into the end of the bobby pin.
3 Turn the pin until the paper is completely wrapped around it.
4 Slide the roll off the pin and glue the loose end.
5 For a small coil leave the paper tightly wound and for a larger one allow it to unwind.

Eyes and teardrops

1 Make a small round coil.
2 Pinch at one end to make a teardrop and at both ends to make an eye.

Scrolls and hearts

1 To make a scroll use a standard round coil left unglued.
2 Unroll it, leave the middle unwound and re-roll the ends.
3 To make a heart, make the scroll and pinch it into a point in the middle.

Stained-glass bottles and glasses

What you need

bottles, jars or glasses
black felt-tipped pen
varnish or lacquer
cellophane
brush

What to do

1 Draw your design onto the glass with a felt-tipped pen.
2 Coat with varnish.
3 Whilst wet, lay your ready-cut pieces of cellophane onto the spaces drawn.
4 Now seal the entire design with another coat of varnish.

12

masks
and
puppets

Aim:

Children of all ages will practise designing, modelling, painting, sewing and gluing through the puppet-building experience.

Objectives:
- To consolidate design skills through the embellishment of masks and puppets.
- To create from scraps a useful tool in the classroom for communication.
- To make children familiar with manipulating materials in a pleasing way.

Puppets can be used in the classroom as a tool for communication. Inventing stories for the puppets to act out is an important experience for children.

Stick puppets

What you need

cardboard
drawing tools
scraps
ice-block stick
glue

What to do

1 Design your puppet on cardboard and embellish it with fabric remnants etc.
2 Cut out around this and mount it onto the ice-block stick.

Shadow puppets

What you need

dark paper
dark drinking-straws or sticks

What to do

1 Design the shape of your puppet on the lighter side of the paper.
2 Hold this up to the light to see that the silhouette you are cutting is a recognisable shape.
3 Cut it out and mount it onto your straw.
4 Shine some light on the puppets so they cast a shadow. An overhead projector is useful in this activity.

Facecloths

What you need

facecloth
needle and thread
felt
other material scraps

What to do

1 Sew the facecloth sides together leaving only a space for your hand.
2 Cut out your character's features and hair from remnants and sew these on.

This one makes a nice gift.

Wraprounds

What you need

paper
scissors
pens
tape

What to do

1 Cut out a semi-circle approximately 6 cm in diameter.
2 Design the character you wish to have.
3 Cut it out and glue it onto the middle of the semi-circle.
4 Curve the semi-circle back around your finger and secure with tape.

Glove puppets

What you need

strong paper or material
fabric remnants
buttons etc
pens
glue
tape or needle and thread

What to do

1 Lay your hand on two
   thicknesses of whatever main
   material you are using,
   positioning your thumb and little
   finger away from the rest of
   your fingers.
2 Trace around larger than your
   hand so that you can have a
   seam.
3 Attach the two together, leaving
   the bottom open for your hand.
4 Embellish with materials at hand.

Brown paper-bag puppets

What you need

brown paper bags
felt
coloured paper-scraps
glue
scissors

What to do

1 Fold the base of the bag down
   flat to form an open and shut
   mouth.
2 Design the face using materials
   at hand.
3 Cut out holes where your eyes
   will be.

Plaster-bandage masks

What you need

plaster of Paris bandages
vaseline
water
paint

What to do

1 Cover your face with vaseline.
2 Cut the bandages into strips of about 5 cm long and 1½ cm wide.
3 Soak the bandages in water for a few seconds to soften the plaster.
4 Layer the bandages onto the face. They will dry within a few minutes.
5 Lift the mask off the face and paint or decorate.

Sock puppets

What you need

old socks
fabric remnants
buttons and sequins
PVA glue

What to do

1 Fill the sock with paper to prevent gluing through both sides.
2 Glue and sew on any materials you have to create your puppet.

Cotton-reel marionettes

What you need

string
two rods or sticks about the same length
felt-tipped pens
fabric remnants
sequins
cotton-reels
(If cotton-reels are unobtainable cut up toilet-roll tubes into sections and paint them.)

What to do

1 Thread about six reels on one string for the neck, head and body.
2 Cut out two cardboard hands and punch holes in the palms.
3 Thread a hand and about three reels for each arm and tie these on at the neck.
4 Cut out the feet or shoes and punch holes in these also.
5 Thread the feet and about four reels for each leg and tie these on to the end of the body.
6 Now cross the sticks and secure tightly in the middle.
7 Drop string from the four ends of the cross and attach the four limbs to these.

Any limbed puppet may be used.

Paperplaters

What you need

paper plate
scissors
pens, crayons etc
ribbons or elastic

What to do

1 Hold the plate up to your face and ask a friend to mark a spot for your eyes, nose and mouth.
2 Cut these out.
3 Embellish the mask to create the character you want.
4 Measure out the amount of elastic or ribbon you need and attach it to the sides of the mask.

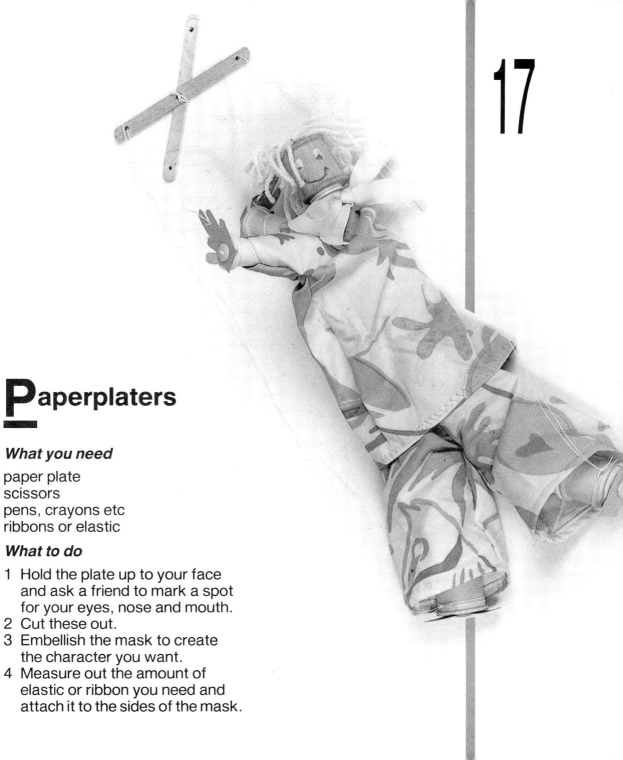

sculpture

Aims:

Here the children will have the opportunity to explore the unique qualities of each modelling media.

They will discover what materials can do when forms are developed and joined together.

Students will become proficient in making aesthetic judgments regarding their work.

Objective:

■ To gain skill in manipulating and joining materials together.

Some terms regarding sculpture

Relief: work which is raised above the surface on which it is modelled.

Mobile: a three-dimensional design which is suspended and free flowing.

Stabile: a mobile which is attached to a base or stand.

Casting: done in a mould and gives an impression.

Biscuit monsters

What you need

large mixing bowl
measuring cups and spoons
biscuit tray
vanilla biscuit mixture

What to do

1 Once the dough has been chilled, divide it into portions and colour each with different food colourings.
2 Roll the dough in your hands until it is soft enough to mould.
3 Model the dough into creatures and place it on the biscuit tray with enough space for expansion.
4 Bake for about ten minutes at 190°C.

Dough sculpture

What you need

inedible dough (see recipe file)
paint
varnish

What to do

1 Knead the dough until soft.
2 Model your one- or two-dimensional sculptures.
3 Make sure you work on wax-paper to make it easy to separate.
4 Allow to dry for a few days or bake for two hours at 150°C.
5 Paint or lacquer.

Soap sculpture

What you need

cake of plain soap
small knife or carving tool
water

What to do

1 Scratch the shape you wish to sculpt onto the face of the soap.
2 Chisel and carve away from those lines to reveal the shape.
3 Smooth the edges by gently rubbing with wet fingers.

Toothpicks and marshmallows

What you need

box of toothpicks
marshmallows (peas are also good)

What to do

1 Use food dye to colour the toothpick first if you don't want the natural colour.
2 Begin by inserting the toothpicks into the marshmallows (or peas).
3 Continue in this manner until your sculpture is done.
4 Eat and enjoy!

Foil sculpture

What you need

kitchen foil
clear tape
paints
wire for bigger models

What to do

1 Crunch up the pieces of foil and form shapes for your creature or model.
2 Attach together with sticky tape.
3 Paint or embellish with remnants.
4 Wire can be used as an internal support structure for larger work.

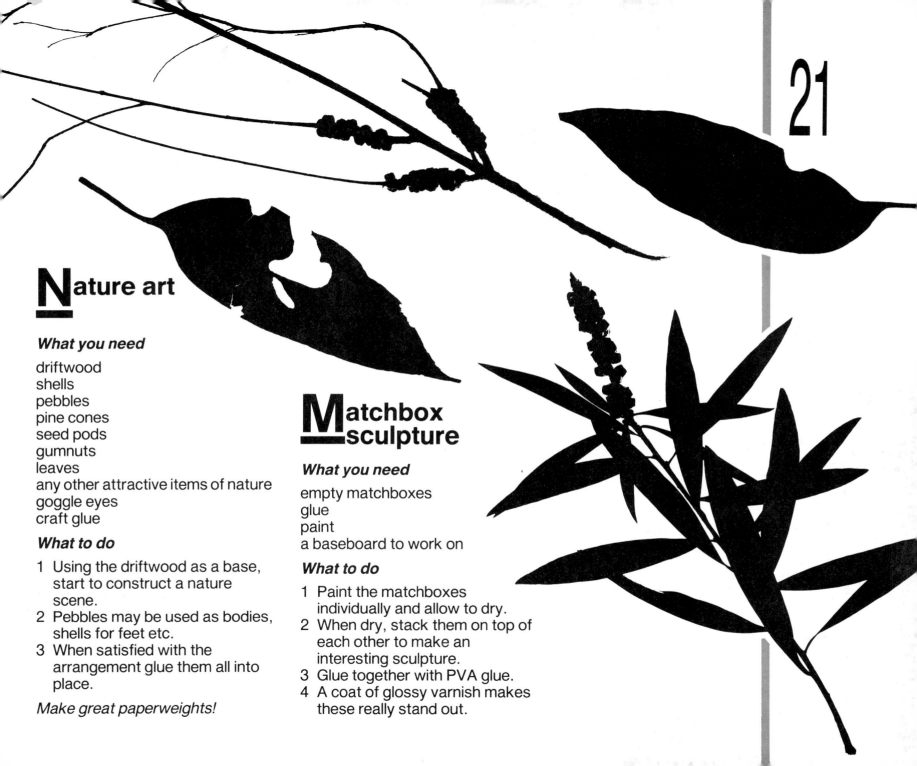

Nature art

What you need

driftwood
shells
pebbles
pine cones
seed pods
gumnuts
leaves
any other attractive items of nature
goggle eyes
craft glue

What to do

1 Using the driftwood as a base, start to construct a nature scene.
2 Pebbles may be used as bodies, shells for feet etc.
3 When satisfied with the arrangement glue them all into place.

Make great paperweights!

Matchbox sculpture

What you need

empty matchboxes
glue
paint
a baseboard to work on

What to do

1 Paint the matchboxes individually and allow to dry.
2 When dry, stack them on top of each other to make an interesting sculpture.
3 Glue together with PVA glue.
4 A coat of glossy varnish makes these really stand out.

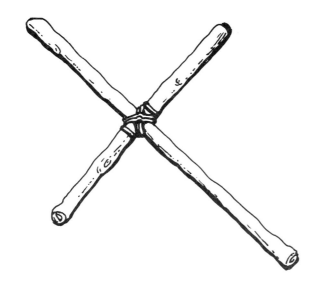

Basic kite

What you need

2 firm sticks
sticky tape
string
paper or plastic
decorative materials

What to do

1 Tie the sticks firmly into a 't' shape with string.
2 Attach string from the tips of the arms to the base to form a triangle. Make sure that the string is pulled as tightly as possible.
3 Cut out the paper around this shape leaving about a 10 cm overlap all the way around.
4 Fold the overlap over the frame and tape down on the inside, trimming the corners as you go.
5 Make a tail from scraps and remnants or bows, approximately three times the length of the kite.
6 Attach and fly.

Grocery-bag kites

What you need

grocery bags
string
decorations for the tail
felt-tip pens
paints etc
stapler

What to do

1 Decorate the bag to be used with collage materials or paints and felt-tip pens.
2 Tie the handles together and attach the string.
3 Make tail pieces and attach these to the top of the bag with a stapler.

*Some interesting
stick arrangements
for kites*

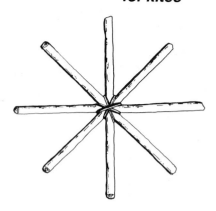

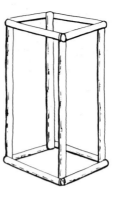

Rectangular fighter

What you need

4 sticks
material
string
needle and thread or glue

What to do

1 Tie the four sticks together firmly with string to form a rectangle.
2 Cut the material larger than the rectangle. Overlap and sew or glue down as in the basic 't' kite.
3 Cut a hole in the centre to allow the air to pass through.
4 Attach four pieces of string, equal in length, to the corners and secure in the middle.

NB: Why not use collage materials and applique to make your kite material?

Glass-jar snow-scenes

What you need

eggshells
coconut or rice
jar with a lid
collage materials from nature, eg
small twigs, gumnuts, pebbles,
pine-cones etc
glue
mineral oil

What to do

1 If using eggshells for snow,
  crush them finely.
2 Paint or cover the lid with
  material.
3 On the inside of the lid, arrange
  the objects and glue them down.
  Decorate the twig branches to
  make them look like trees.
4 Fill the jar with mineral oil when
  dry and add the crushed
  eggshells or coconut.
5 Screw the lid on firmly and give
  it a gentle shake.
6 Now turn the jar upside down
  and watch the snow slowly
  falling.

People puzzles

What you need

large magazine pictures or photos
of family and friends
cardboard
glue
clear contact/optional
scissors or Stanley knife

What to do

1 Glue the photo onto heavy
  cardboard and contact it for
  protection if you wish.
2 Turn it over and draw some
  puzzle shapes on the back of
  the cardboard.
3 Cut up the puzzle.

*NB: If you have a photo of a friend,
you might like to cut it up and give
it to them as a gift.*

33

What to do

1 Slide the stick of the dish mop through the lemon, making sure that the pointed bottom becomes the witch's nose. The mop will form the hair.
2 Make a dress by cutting two shapes as in diagram, making sure it is long enough to cover the stick.
3 Curve the dress around and glue it together.
4 Decorate and add a face to the witch.

Beanbag friends

What you need

old gloves, mittens and socks
marking pens and collage materials
large needle and wool
beans or rice
PVA glue

What to do

1 Use the collage materials to decorate a glove or mitten (buttons are always good for eyes).
2 Fill the mitten with beans or rice. Try not to fill it too tightly.
3 Sew the edge up with strong cotton or yarn.

Dishmop witch

What you need

dishmop
lemon, potato or apple for the head
black cardboard or felt
glue
glitter or spray paint
gummed stars
scissors

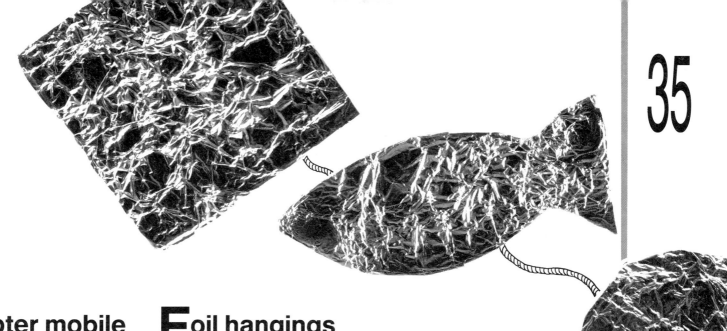

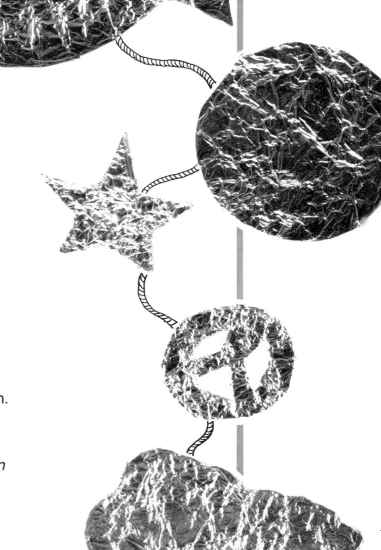

Helicopter mobile

What you need

egg-cartons
glue
scissors
crayons
paint
cardboard

What to do

1 Helicopters consist of two
  eggcups glued together.
2 Cut out windows in the top
  eggcup.
3 Glue the tail and propellers, or a
  pin can be used for moving
  blades.
4 If you wish you can also attach
  cardboard feet.
5 Suspend in the same way as the
  fish mobile.

Foil hangings

What you need

silver, gold and coloured foils
cardboard
scissors
glue
cotton
sticks

What to do

1 Draw a design onto cardboard
  and cut these pieces out
  through two layers of foil.
2 Glue the foil to the front and
  back placing thread in between.
3 Attach to the sticks and hang.

*NB: If you wish to make patterns
on the foil, lay the pieces down on
a soft surface and push patterns
into it with a pencil.*

Designer tiles

What you need

clay
leaves
scratching implements
rolling pin
damp scrap material
ruler
scissors or knife

What to do

1 Knead and wedge the clay to remove air bubbles.
2 Spread the damp cloth out on the working surface and weight it down.
3 Roll out the clay to approximately 2 cm thickness and cut into a square.
4 Design a pattern on paper the same size as the tile and allow the tile to dry out to leather hard.
5 Scratch your design into the tile, cutting away areas if you wish.
6 Allow to dry. Fire and glaze.

Pinchpot

What you need

clay

What to do

1 Knead or wedge the clay to remove any air bubbles.
2 Roll into a smooth ball approximately the size of an orange.
3 Whilst holding the ball in the fingers of both hands, press thumbs into the ball forming a pot upside down.
4 Continue pressing while rotating the ball to form the pot.
5 Smooth out any cracks with damp fingers and give the pot a flat base by tapping it gently on the table.
6 Allow to dry slowly at room temperature before firing and glazing.

48

Penholders

What you need

clay
pens
rolling pin/optional

What to do

1 Knead and wedge the clay to remove air bubbles.

2 Shape the clay into an animal or object of your choice, making sure there is enough room on the surface to put pencil holes.
3 Using the pens, push holes into the back of the animal or object, making sure that they are deep enough to hold them.
4 Allow to dry. Fire and glaze.

Owl wall-hangings

What you need

clay
string
rolling pin
knife

What to do

1 Knead and wedge the clay to remove any air bubbles.
2 Roll out the clay to approximately 1 to 1½ cm thickness.
3 Cut a shape out which resembles an oval.
4 Fold the top flap down to form the owl's face, laying a piece of string under it to hang it up by.
5 Form feathers around the base of the owl by pinching it, and use a knife to carve the eyes in. Pinch up a nose.
6 Allow to dry at room temperature before hanging.

NB: It is not necessary to fire these.

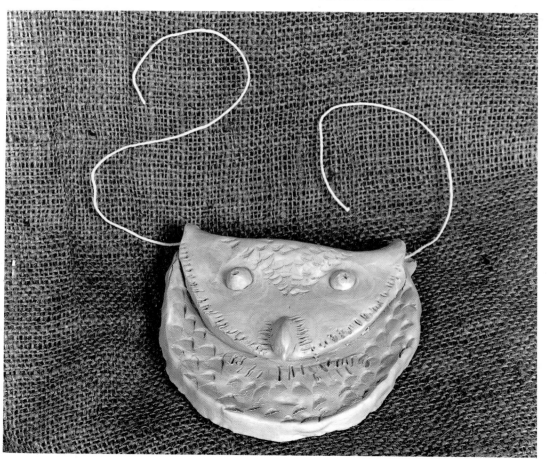

Dough picture frames

What you need

bread dough (see recipe file)
knife
ruler
stiff cardboard

What to do

1 Roll the dough out to approximately 1 cm thickness and large enough for a rectangle the size of the frame.
2 Cut out the cardboard backing as well as the dough front.
3 Cut the shape out of dough for the photograph.
4 With the scraps cut out from the centre, decorate the frame.
5 Bake in a moderate oven and paint or varnish.
6 Glue the backing onto the dough, leaving the bottom open to insert a photo.

Dough baskets

What you need

greased oven-proof dish
bread dough (see recipe file)
eggwhite

What to do

1 Roll the dough into long, thin strips.
2 Weave the strips over the dish.
3 Bake in a moderate oven for forty-five minutes.
4 Remove the dish, brush with eggwhite and join on a plaited strip to make the rim.
5 Return to the oven for a further thirty minutes.
6 Varnish when cool.

Coil bowls

What you need

clay rolled into coils
bowls or pots
cloth or gladwrap

What to do

1 If using a bowl to shape from, first line with gladwrap or cloth to prevent sticking.
2 Roll coils thinly and begin lining the inside of the bowl with them until you reach the top.
3 Carefully smooth the sides down to join and disguise the coils. Do this very lightly so as not to spoil the coils on the outside.
4 Allow the bowl to dry until it slowly and easily slips out from the bowl.
5 Allow to dry. Fire and glaze if desired.

Pretzel sculpture

What you need

pretzel dough (see recipe file)
egg yolk
salt
water

What to do

1 Roll the dough into a smooth modelling texture.
2 Shape the dough into forms, animals and designs.
3 Brush with an egg yolk diluted with water and sprinkle with salt.
4 Bake at approximately 200°C for twenty minutes.

Flower holders

What you need

clay
newspaper
cutting implement
textures/optional

What to do

1 Knead and wedge the clay then flatten it into a large oval shape approximately 25 cm long.
2 Fold this in half and cut through the fold so that you have two pieces on top of each other.
3 Add textures to the top surface if you wish (lightly pressing hessian into it will make a nice design).
4 Pinch the edges together and place a hole at both corners for the string.
5 Fire and glaze.

How to make use of those paper bags, plates and cups

paper-cup bell decoration

pop-up people

paper-plate object holder

paper-bag clothes

paper-bag masks

telephones

Box sculpture

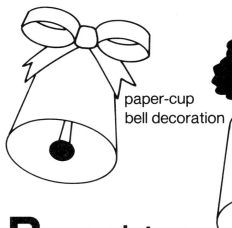

What you need

cardboard boxes and tubes
paint
tape or glue
wool
string
collage materials

What to do

1 Tape cardboard boxes and tubes together to make various sculptures.
2 Paint and decorate the sculptures.
3 Join together several sculptures by using string, and suspend from the ceiling.

maracas (2 cups and an ice-block stick)

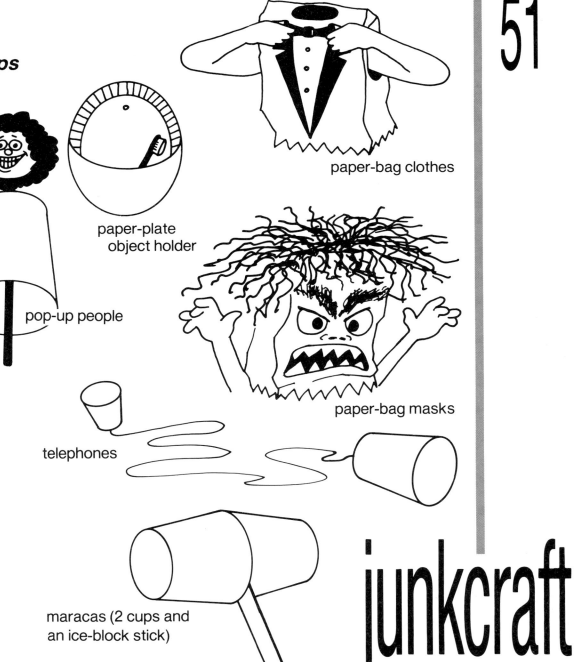

junkcraft

Pencil holders

What you need

empty soup cans
scissors
glue
collage materials
cardboard

What to do

1 Make sure there is no paper or glue on the can before you begin.
2 Decide on a character or animal to convert the can into.
3 Using the collage materials, cut out ears, hair and other features needed for the character.
4 Glue or tape them on.

Hanging tidy

What you need

milk container
string
glue
tape
scissors
paint
fabric scraps

What to do

1 Cut away the top of the milk container and cut open the carton as shown.
2 Fold back the sides to make a triple thickness backing to hang by.
3 Paint the tidy with poster paint or decorate it yourself with fabric scraps or remnants.
4 Punch a hole at the top and thread with ribbon or string to hang.

Egg people

What you need

egg
needle
paint, felt-tipped pens
collage materials

What to do

1 Warm the egg on a window-ledge in the sun until you are ready to use it.

2 Use the needle to make a small hole at each end of the egg (one hole should be slightly larger than the other).

3 Blow into the smaller hole until all the egg has left the shell through the larger hole.

4 Carefully wash and dry the egg.

5 Decorate the egg using felt-tipped pens, paint, etc. You could draw faces or attach hair.

Easter-egg birds

What you need

hard-boiled eggs
paper
craft glue
dye bath
paint

What to do

1 Dye a hard-boiled egg (see 'Egg-dyeing', this section).

2 Using either plain or patterned paper, fanfold two small pieces of paper for wings and an even smaller one for the tail.

3 Attach these to the egg with tape or glue.

4 Paint on a face.

Egg tree

What you need

branches
pots of sand
paint/optional

What to do

1 Find an attractive branch and strip it of its leaves.

2 Stand the branch in a pot of sand.

3 Either spray paint the branch or leave it natural.

4 Hang your decorated eggs on the tree.

Collage Easter eggs

What you need

hard-boiled eggs
collage materials
PVA glue

What to do

1 Coat the eggs with glue.

2 Decorate them with Easter scenes and symbols using the collage materials available.

Happy Easter

Easter-egg card

What you need

template H
coloured pencils, felt-tipped pens
scissors

What to do

1. Decorate the Easter egg.

2. Fold the page along the dotted line.

3. Cut out around the edges of the egg, being very careful not to cut the fold that makes the card.

4. Write your Easter message inside.

Easter-bunny card

What you need

template I
coloured pencils, felt-tipped pens
scissors

What to do

1. Decorate the card as you wish.

2. Cut around the edges and along the outside dotted lines.

3. Fold along the inside dotted lines to make the card.

4. Write your message inside.

Christmas mobiles

What you need

a variety of wrapping papers
cardboard
glue
scissors
fishing line or string
Christmas shape templates

What to do

1 Use the templates or design your own to transfer onto cardboard.
2 Cut squares of paper large enough to cover the shapes and glue up one side.
3 Carefully cut out the shapes.
4 Now glue the other piece on to the back and carefully trim.
5 Punch a hole and thread these together into a mobile or Christmas decorations for the tree.

NB: the shapes provided were drawn from biscuit cutters. They make easy stencils.

christmas
collection

Scrap pictures

What you need

material remnants
Christmas wrapping paper
Christmas collage materials
scissors
glue
pencils
cardboard

What to do

1 Draw a Christmas design on the cardboard.

2 Arrange the materials as you wish to place them.

3 Glue them on to your design.

Orange-bag stockings

What you need

orange bags
scissors
glue
pens, pencils, etc
magazines, gift catalogues
backing paper

What to do

1 Cut items from magazines that you would like to find in your Christmas stocking.

2 Glue these onto the backing paper.

3 Cover this with a piece of orange bag cut into the shape of a stocking.

Paper-plate Santas

What you need

2 paper plates
red cardboard
felt-tipped pens
glue, tape
scissors

What to do

1 Cut away the edges of the paper plates and construct Santa's beard by fastening them together with glue or tape.

2 Using the circular part of a plate for the face, insert plate edging for the eyebrows and moustache.

3 Cut two small red cardboard circles for the cheeks and paste these onto the face.

4 Glue on the beard.

5 Cut out a hat from the red cardboard and use paper plate edging for the ruffle and pompom on the hat.

6 Hang.

Origami Christmas tree

What you need

coloured squares of paper
Christmas wrapping paper
scissors

What to do

1 Fold the paper diagonally in half.

2 Fold again, making sure the centre point is at the top.

3 Cut alternately from side to side and stop approximately 1 cm from the top.

4 Open and decorate with wrapping-paper cut-outs.

5 Hang.

Padded mobiles

What you need

Christmas-print fabrics
glue
cardboard
wadding or padding
fishing line

What to do

1 Using the templates provided or your own designs, cut out carefully.
2 Glue down thin wadding or foam and trim.
3 Stretch the fabric tightly over the foam and glue to the back.
4 Using a cut-out of the same shape, cover with fabric.
5 Glue the two shapes together evenly to hide the edges.
6 When the required number of shapes are completed, string together to make a wall centrepiece or mobile.

Material or wrapping-paper wreaths

What you need

fabric or wrapping-paper prints
cardboard
glue
scissors
templates
pressure tape/optional

What to do

1 Decide on the shapes that you wish to have in your wreath (it is a good idea not to use too many but to repeat the same shape).
2 Cover the shapes using the same procedure as for Christmas mobiles.
3 Arrange the shapes in a circle, slightly overlapping. Remember to alternate the shapes in sequence.
4 Attach each shape, right-hand top corner to the bottom of the next shape, until you have completed the wreath.

Padded Christmas greetings

What you need

wadding or foam
fabric scraps
craft glue
alphabet templates
scissors

What to do

1 Decide on the message or greeting you wish to make and cut out the appropriate letters.
2 Glue the wadding or foam to the letters and trim.
3 Pull the fabric tightly over the letters, trim and glue to the back.
4 These can either be glued to a fabric-coated backing board or mounted and arranged on the wall as they are.

Nature wreath

What you need

pine cones, nuts, berries, varnished apples, leaves, holly etc
PVA glue
Christmas playdough or florists' putty
cardboard
scissors

What to do

1 Draw a large circle and a smaller one inside to form the base for the wreath. Cut out.
2 Apply dough generously around the circle.
3 Arrange the objects strategically and press firmly into the dough. If you are using real fruit, a few coats of varnish will preserve them for approximately six to eight weeks.

NB: this makes a lovely table centrepiece with candles placed in the middle.

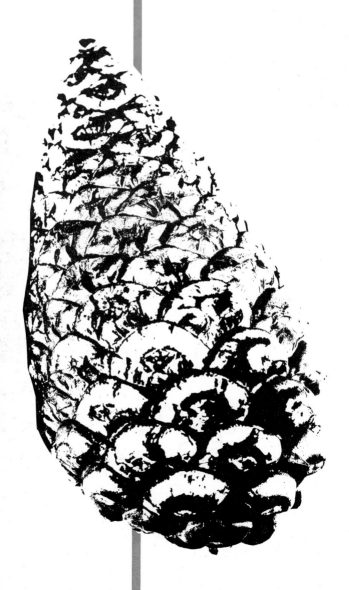

Patchwork balls

What you need

styrofoam balls
Stanley knife
fabric scraps
ribbon
ice-block sticks

What to do

1 Decide on a pattern for the ball. Segmenting it like an orange is the easiest way to start off.
2 Draw the pattern onto the ball with pencil as a guide for cutting.
3 With a craft knife, cut into the ball where the lines are, approximately 5 mm in depth.
4 Cut your fabric into pieces 1 cm larger (all around) than the shapes you have cut into the ball.
5 Using an ice-block stick, gently push the fabric into the grooves you have made, and trim any necessary edges as you go.
6 To hang, push a pin through both ends of a small ribbon to form a loop. Push this pin firmly into the ball and hang.

Patchwork tree quilt

What you need

Christmas fabric
wadding or foam
needle and thread
lace and ribbon/optional
scissors

What to do

1 Cut your fabric into squares 11 cm x 11 cm. You will need a hundred for a large skirt.
2 Draw up 1 cm margins around these as a sewing line if necessary.
3 Join together five rows of ten squares making strips. Then sew these five rows together to form the top half of the quilt, fifty squares remaining.
4 Join five squares together to make ten half-length rows.
5 Join these rows up to make two bottom sections to the quilt. The split it forms to the centre will allow the stem of the tree to sit inside.
6 Attach these to the top half of the quilt and cut out a piece of fabric equal in size to the backing.
7 Sew together.

Christmas puddings

What you need

balloons (round)
wire
calico or white linen
Christmas ribbon
pine cones and decorations
scissors
craft glue

What to do

1 Blow the balloon up to about half size or a nice size for a pudding.
2 Cut a piece of material approximately three times the size of the balloon in the shape of a square.
3 Paint the balloon with a layer of craft glue.
4 Place the balloon in the centre of the material and carefully gather up all four corners, smoothing the fabric onto the balloon as you go.
5 Twist the wire tightly around the top and tie bright Christmas ribbon over it.
6 Add any decorations you wish at the top near the bow, and hang with Christmas ribbon.

Wire bell

What you need

thin wire (modelling)
lace
ribbon
small bell decorations and trimmings
masking tape
craft glue
pine cones

What to do

1 Shape a long piece of modelling wire into the form of a bell.
2 Tear off strips of masking tape and wrap these continuously over the wire to conceal it.
3 Using craft glue, attach lace around the shape.
4 Thread a piece of ribbon through the loop at the top of the bell and suspend this by tying at the top of the wire shape.
5 Dress the top with pine cones, ribbon etc.

Matchstick shapes

What you need

wax-paper
matchsticks
craft knife/scissors
paint
wood glue

What to do

1 Choose a Christmas decoration
shape to make.

2 Draw the shape onto wax-paper.

3 Fill in the shape by gluing on cut
matchsticks.

4 Leave it to dry before lifting off
the wax-paper.

5 Paint or leave natural.

6 Attach a piece of string and hang.

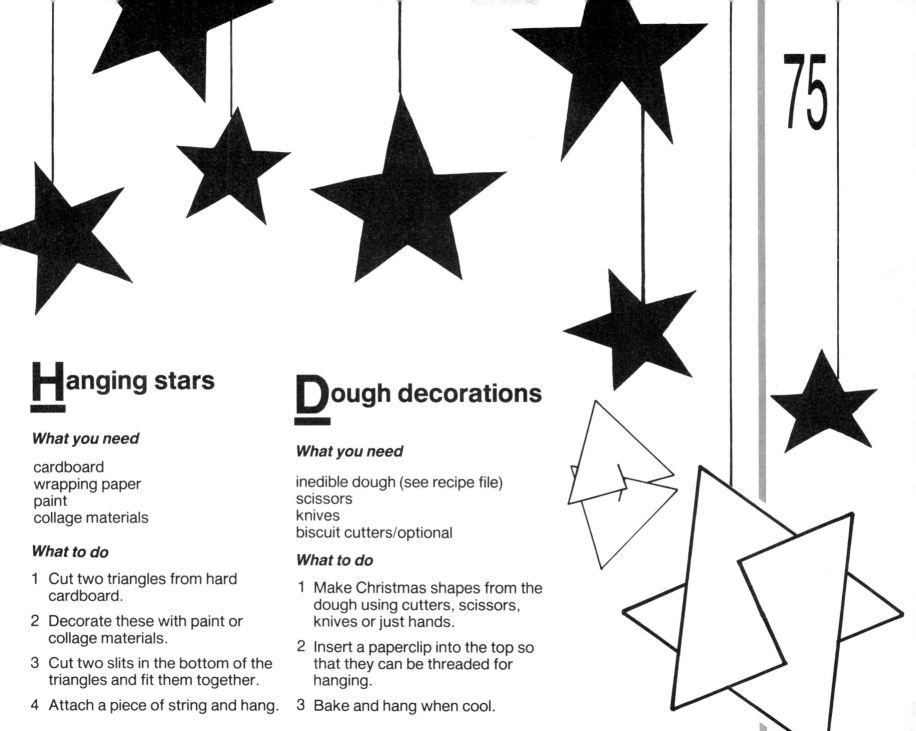

Hanging stars

What you need

cardboard
wrapping paper
paint
collage materials

What to do

1 Cut two triangles from hard cardboard.

2 Decorate these with paint or collage materials.

3 Cut two slits in the bottom of the triangles and fit them together.

4 Attach a piece of string and hang.

Dough decorations

What you need

inedible dough (see recipe file)
scissors
knives
biscuit cutters/optional

What to do

1 Make Christmas shapes from the dough using cutters, scissors, knives or just hands.

2 Insert a paperclip into the top so that they can be threaded for hanging.

3 Bake and hang when cool.

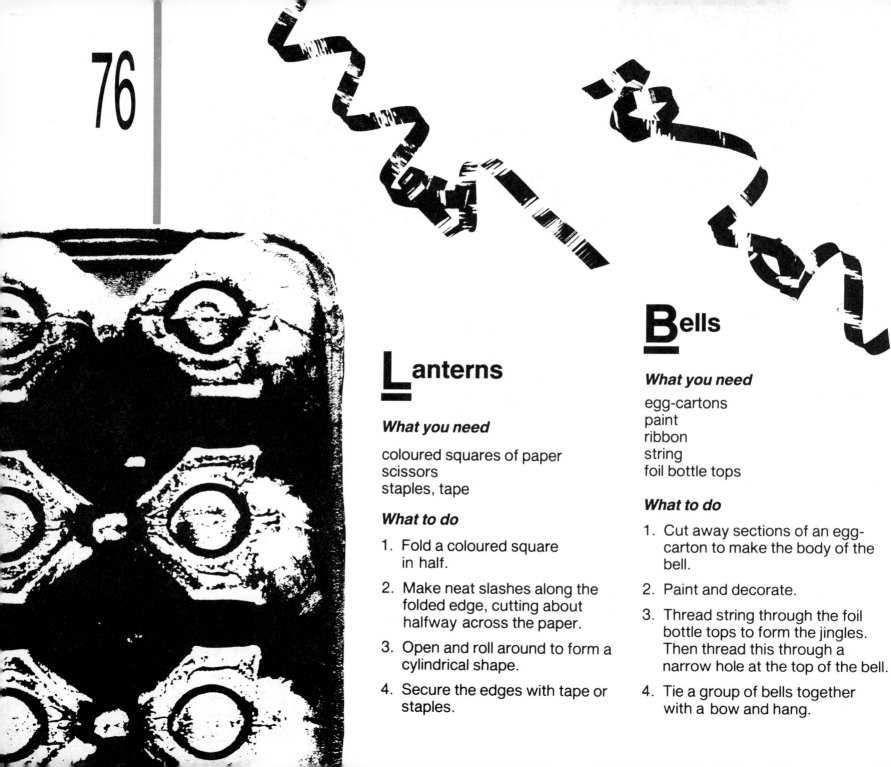

Lanterns

What you need

coloured squares of paper
scissors
staples, tape

What to do

1. Fold a coloured square in half.

2. Make neat slashes along the folded edge, cutting about halfway across the paper.

3. Open and roll around to form a cylindrical shape.

4. Secure the edges with tape or staples.

Bells

What you need

egg-cartons
paint
ribbon
string
foil bottle tops

What to do

1. Cut away sections of an egg-carton to make the body of the bell.

2. Paint and decorate.

3. Thread string through the foil bottle tops to form the jingles. Then thread this through a narrow hole at the top of the bell.

4. Tie a group of bells together with a bow and hang.

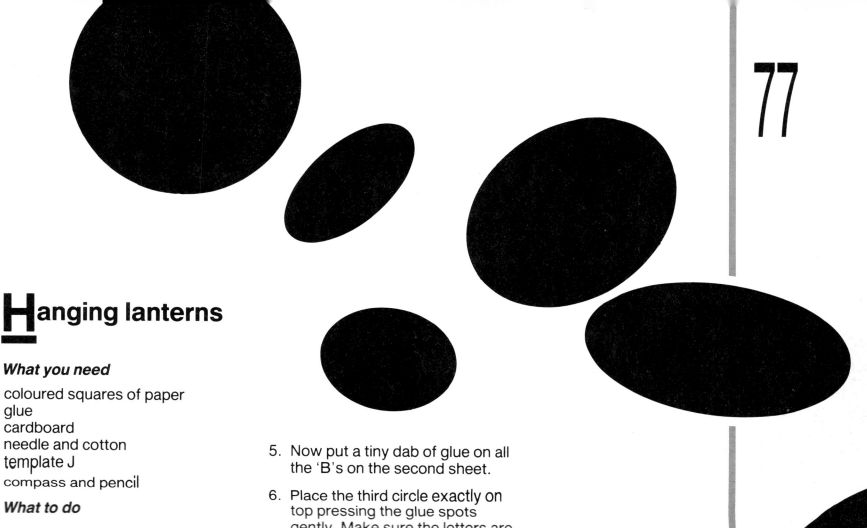

Hanging lanterns

What you need

coloured squares of paper
glue
cardboard
needle and cotton
template J
compass and pencil

What to do

1. Cut out thirty circles using template J.

2. Using a compass, label each circle as on the template.

3. Put a tiny dab of glue on all the 'A's on the first circle.

4. Place the next circle exactly on top with the letters facing you. Gently press where the glue spots are.

5. Now put a tiny dab of glue on all the 'B's on the second sheet.

6. Place the third circle exactly on top pressing the glue spots gently. Make sure the letters are facing you.

7. Continue in this manner until all the circles have been used.

8. Place a cardboard circle on the top and bottom and allow to dry.

9. Carefully pull open to give an accordion effect.

10. Thread the top with cotton and hang.

Name:

_____

Template H

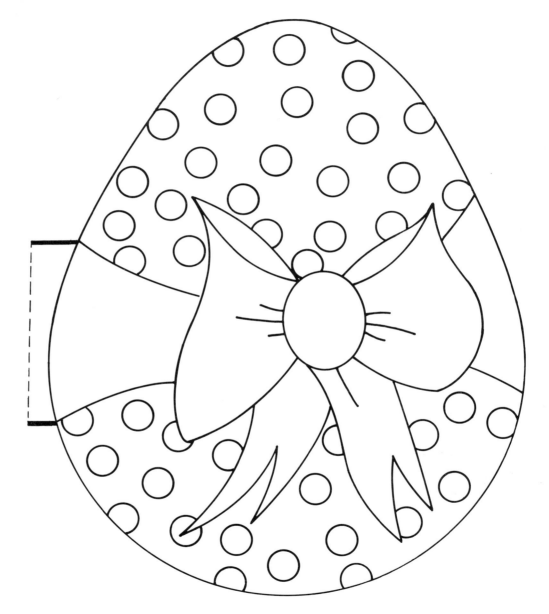

Template J

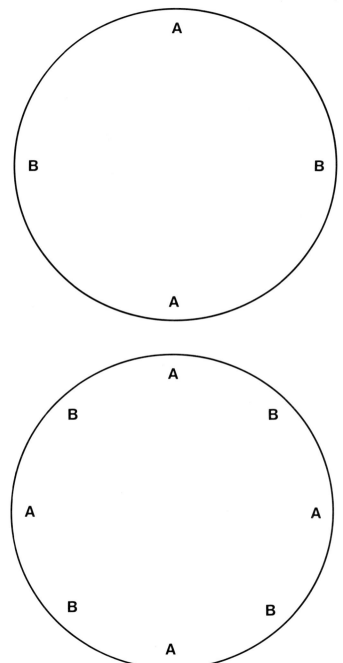

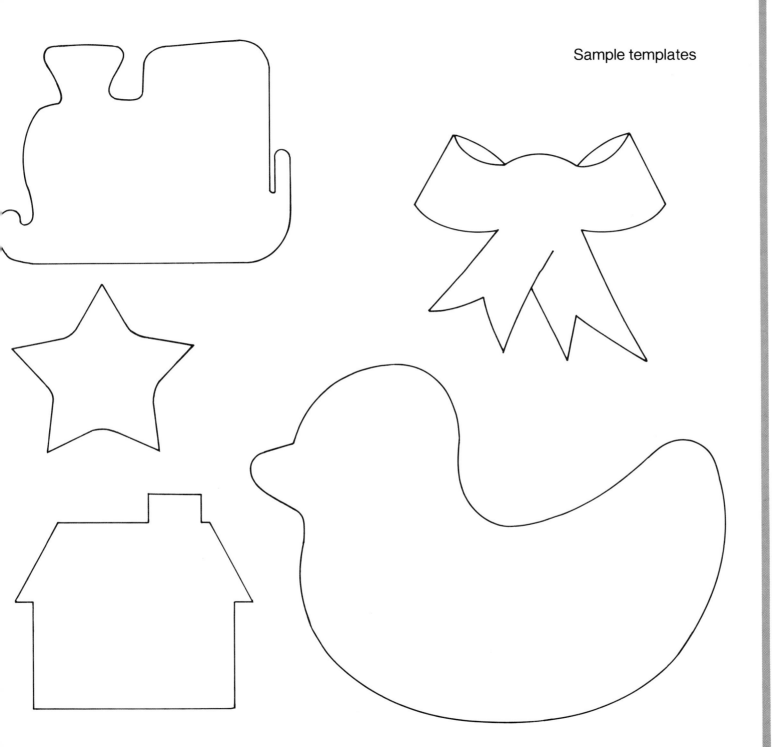

Sample templates

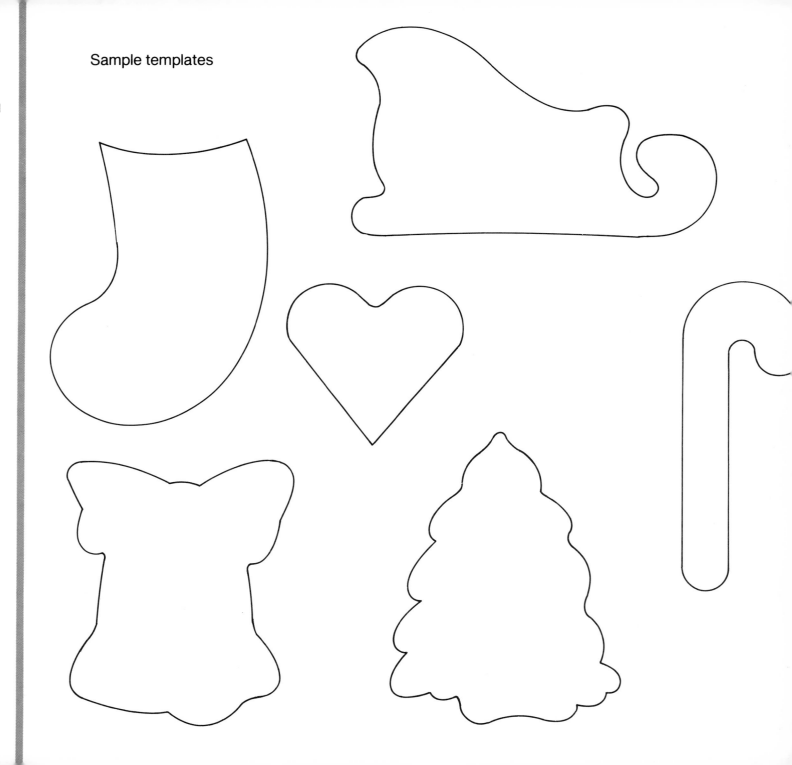

notes